harbor

Hello!

I'm Tom. Every weekend, I come to the harbor. I buy an ice cream, and I watch the boats.

I put some money in the coin-binoculars.
Then, I can see the boats very well.

The harbor is an interesting place. There are
boats of all shapes and sizes. And they all do
different things.

I can show you ...

Here's the ferry! Can you see the people? The ferry is taking them from that side of the harbor to this side.

Some people take the ferry to work. Some people take their bicycles on the ferry. That's smart!

NORTHCOTT
SYDNEY

ferry

RAHNCH

tugboat

What's this? It's a tugboat, and it's pulling a big boat. Can you see the rope between the two boats?

The tugboat is moving slowly. The big boat is heavy, but that's OK — tugboats are very strong!

What's that?

Oh ... it's a speedboat, and a woman
is wakeboarding!

speedboat

wakeboard

wake

The wake is the shape of the water behind the boat.

The woman is standing on the wakeboard, and the speedboat is pulling her. She's very good!

Look! Here are some sailing boats. It's windy today in the harbor. This is good for the sailing boats. The sails catch the wind, and the boats move quickly.

sail

sailing boat

I'm in the sailing club at school – I love it!

police boat

What's that? A police boat is speeding toward that fishing boat!

The fishing boat is stopping. The police are speaking to the men on the boat.

That's an interesting job! The harbor police are important.

fishing boat

Goodbye!

It's true – the harbor is an interesting place. But now it's time to take the ferry home.

Activities

Before You Read

1 Match the pictures of the boats to the words.

> ferry   tugboat   speedboat
> sailing boat   police boat   fishing boat

(a)

(b)

(c)

(d)

(e)

(f)

After You Read

1 Read and write Yes (Y) or No (N).

1 Some people take the ferry to work.

2 Tugboats are not strong.

3 Sailing boats can move quickly.

4 Harbor police are important.

5 The harbor is not an interesting place.

2 Which is your favorite boat from the book?
Draw a picture of it.

Pearson Education Limited
Edinburgh Gate, Harlow,
Essex CM20 2JE, England
and Associated Companies throughout the world.

ISBN: 978-1-4479-4434-8

This edition first published by Pearson Education Ltd 2013
3 5 7 9 10 8 6 4 2
Text copyright © Pearson Education Ltd 2013

The moral rights of the author have been asserted
in accordance with the Copyright Designs and Patents Act 1988

Set in 19/23pt OT Fiendstar Semibold
Printed in China
SWTC/02

Acknowledgements
The publisher would like to thank the following for their kind permission to reproduce their photographs:
(Key: b-bottom; c-center; l-left; r-right; t-top)

Alamy Images: Chad Ehlers 1, Oleksiy Maksymenko 8-9, 15 (a), Rick Piper Photography 12, 15 (b),
Transport Picture Library / Paul Ridsdale 15 (c), Charles Stirling 5-6; **Fotolia.com:** Benmm 2-3,
James Clarke 15 (f); **Getty Images:** Rob Elliott / Stringer 13; **PhotoDisc:** Photolink 10-11, 15 (e);
Shutterstock.com: Max Earey 4-5, Reinhold Leitner 14, Max Lindenthaler 15 (d)
Cover images: Front: Alamy Images: AWPhoto

All other images © Pearson Education

In some instances we have been unable to trace the owners of copyright material,
and we would appreciate any information that would enable us to do so.

Illustrations: Mike Brownlow

Published by Pearson Education Ltd

For a complete list of the titles available in the Pearson English Kids Readers series, please go to
www.pearsonenglishkidsreaders.com. Alternatively, write to your local Pearson Education office or to
Pearson English Readers Marketing Department, Pearson Education, Edinburgh Gate, Harlow, Essex CM202JE, England.